CLOSER

A JOURNEY WITH JESUS

FROM HIS LIFE TO YOURS

JEFF LITTLE

Closer
Copyright 2018 Jeff Little

www.milestonechurch.com
ISBN: 978-1-947165-87-8

Printed in the United States.

CONTENTS

Preface

I remember as a young boy hearing the Bible stories that are contained in this book. But at 12 years old, something shifted as these stories became more than just words on a page. They became real to me. Jesus became more than a Bible character, a prophet, or a teacher. He became *my* Jesus and I surrendered my life to Him.

I preached my first sermon at 16 years old and found myself pastoring my first church at the age of 21. Since then, from platforms and stages to living rooms and coffee shops, I've had the opportunity to share Jesus countless times with people.

The venues have changed over the years, but one thing hasn't changed as I prepare to preach each weekend. In the brief moment before the lights come up on stage, I repeat this one simple truth that has carried me through a few decades of ministry: *I'm doing this for You, Jesus.*

You don't build a great life, a great home, or a great church on strategy. You build it on the revelation of Jesus. I first visited the Holy Land as a young pastor in my twenties. When my feet hit the ground in Israel again twenty years later, I had you in mind. As I walked where Jesus walked and visited the locations of some of His most significant moments, I couldn't think of any greater target in writing this book than helping you get closer to Jesus.

I hope through these pages the stories of Jesus come alive to you in a new way. And most importantly, I pray that through the Word of God in the pages of Scripture, you discover a Savior who wants to be close to you.

Jeff Little

Introduction

If strangers from another universe came to Earth and studied human history, eventually they'd compile some sort of a list detailing the most significant people who've ever lived.

And there, in front of kings, presidents, conquerors, global entertainers, genius inventors, and titans of industry would be a carpenter from a small town in Israel who died in His 30s.

He left behind no political empire, business, or even a wife and family as His legacy.

Yet somehow more people have heard and known His name than any other person in recorded human history.

Still today, more than 2,000 years later, nearly 2 billion people around the world say they look to Him for inspiration, direction, and meaning. No other individual has been the subject of so many books, songs, poems, paintings, and films.

Yet despite all His fame and renown, to many people Jesus remains a mystery.

Most people have an opinion of Jesus, but how can we get close to Him?

This is a question we don't want to leave unresolved. We don't want to simply embrace the opinion of a family member, the latest views of college professors, or the loudest person on social media.

Recently a friend shared an interesting experience with me. She'd been traveling all day with her husband, and when they finally reached their hotel she was ready to take off her shoes, put her feet up, and relax.

Like many of us, she'd been so preoccupied with flight times, security lines, rental car arrangements, and all of the rest of the administration of travel, she'd forgotten how hungry she was. As she began to unwind, she noticed a beautiful small bowl of apples waiting for her in the room.

She was thrilled.

This was one of those rare moments when the very thing you're craving happens to be right there waiting for you. The closer she got to the delicious piece of fruit, the higher her anticipation rose. She grabbed a spotless apple, closed her eyes, and took a big bite.

The apple was rotten.

You can almost taste it in your mind right now, because whether or not you've shared a similar experience with fruit, you know this feeling. More than disappointment, it feels like a betrayal of trust. It stays with you.

I have a friend who had one bad experience with mayonnaise and still years later he refuses to eat anything remotely associated with the creamy dressing.

This principle extends beyond food.

When our hopes run high, failed expectations are devastating. They cause us to question whether it's worth putting ourselves out there again. We grow more cautious.

If this prompts us to be more discerning, then the entire process can help us mature in wisdom and understanding. But for most people, these types of moments are painful enough to get them to lose sight of the things in life that matter most.

I've worked with people for a few decades, and I've seen this cycle repeated over and over in some of the most important parts of our lives.

> A bad experience with a teacher early in school causes you to see yourself as dumb and you close off potential opportunities for your future.
>
> A difficult home life with your family leads you to question whether or not it's even possible for a marriage to be healthy and life-giving.
>
> A business venture with a dishonest partner damages your trust to the point where your ability to build your career is severely impaired.
>
> A painful interaction with a mean-spirited, arrogant person who claims to speak on behalf of God convinces you that claims about church, the Bible, or Jesus can't be trusted.

Wisdom and discernment can help us look more carefully, but they can't completely eliminate risk. One of the most fascinating features of our world is how incredible beauty can be found next to unthinkable evil.

The question comes down to our ability to tell the difference. *How do we know which is which?*

We keep our heads up and our eyes open. It all comes down to what we see. Instead of wandering through life, we choose to live intentionally and examine which direction we're heading.

This doesn't mean we take the path of least resistance—not everything that's easy is worth getting closer to. But the closer we get, the more we're able to determine value and worth.

There are people, experiences, and objects in life we mistakenly overlook until we get close enough to discover them for ourselves. At the same time, there is another category we esteem and move toward only to later discover their inability to deliver what we were searching for.

The closer we get, the more inauthentic, the less valuable, the less significant they become. I can't speak for you, but I distance myself from those things.

I'll take less of them, not more.

One of the things I'm wary of is waking up one day to realize I've focused on the wrong things, which moved me to a place I didn't want to go. My goal is to move further away from the things that don't matter so I can truly prioritize the ones that do.

Which brings us back to Jesus.

The closer I get to Jesus, the more valuable He becomes. I always want more, not less.

I grew up in a home where we talked about Him for as long as I can remember. I met Him in a real way when I was 12 years old. I've walked with Him ever since and have given my life to try to help others see and know Him through an authentic, personal relationship.

But He's never boring. He doesn't sit still. When I think I have Him figured out, He becomes way smarter, far more loving, and even more supernatural than the day before.

The goal of this book is not for you to gather information or content in order to prepare for a quiz. Instead, my hope is that as we go on this journey together, you won't just learn about Jesus—but instead you'll grow closer to Him.

When you take this approach, He has a proven track record of jumping off the pages of Scripture and showing up in the most unexpected areas of our lives.

The majority of Jesus' ministry was not event-driven. He would go and live with the people, He would adapt and engage with the rhythms of daily life, and He would bring His disciples with Him.

He didn't lack intention or strategy—this approach was clearly on purpose. We know this because most of the time the disciples had no idea what Jesus was up to, but He was always talking about His Father's plan. Periodically He would stop and explain to them what He was up to and how it would require them to change.

We're going to take this same approach.

I spent a couple of weeks walking through the places where He lived, where He met with real people, where He healed the sick, where He walked on water, where He helped those who felt abandoned and alone experience the peace of God.

My intent was to understand Him more, to get closer to Him, and to not only appreciate what He did then but to be more aware of what He's doing now.

This book can be a stand-alone resource, but if you'd like to see what these locations look like for yourself and supplement what you're learning in the book, I went on location to the scenes and shot a short video. At the start of every chapter, I tell you where I went and I give you the address for the link.[1]

As we move deeper into His life, and take a closer look at some of His most significant moments, my prayer is that you would see Him more clearly.

[1] Videos can be found at closer.milestonechurch.com.

Not just so you can understand His life, but also so He can help you understand yours.

Here's the good news: you can be as close to Jesus as you want. He never turns away any man, woman, or child who comes to Him with a desire to know and love Him more.

The truth is, as we'll discover during the time He walked the earth, He's always moving closer to us. I believe the fact that you're reading these words right now is evidence that this is already happening.

Go ahead. Take a closer look. You may be surprised by what you find.

ONE

Jesus Calls the Disciples

"Come and follow me."

You can watch my video for this chapter from the shore of the Sea of Galilee here: closer.milestonechurch.com

During our adult lives, the average American spends more time at work than anywhere else. And yet, 80 percent of us describe ourselves as "unfulfilled" in our work environment.

This is one of the great existential challenges of our era. Enormous amounts of energy and effort on the part of many gifted and intelligent people are working to resolve this tension.

This is the driving force behind the individual assessment industry, the TED conference, the life-coach movement, and a plethora of best-selling books and podcasts.

There are all kinds of reasons we could cite to further explain this inner turmoil we're wrestling with, but these are perhaps the three most common:

> We're trying to figure out how to resolve the tension between seeking promotions and doing work we genuinely care about.
>
> We're trying to pivot to our ideal role so we can maximize our potential and fully utilize our gifts and abilities.
>
> We're trying to discover the secret to maintaining the ideal work-life balance so we can experience the dual fulfillment of the absolute best career and family that life has to offer at the same time—as soon as we can get it.

Perhaps the most unusual thing about all this is that most Americans look to God to make this possible—but we don't expect Him to actually show up at our workplace.

Since the early '90s we've learned to expect "Take Your Daughter to Work Day." In 2018 we even celebrated the 20th anniversary of "Take Your Dog to Work Day." If you're paying attention, you realize there is no "Take Your Cat to Work Day," because cats are selfish and basically a symbol of pure evil.

If you're keeping score, it's daughters yes, dogs yes, and cats and God no.

When you stop to think about it, we shouldn't be surprised most of us don't feel close to Jesus.

We're trying to keep up with the demands of work, we have all kinds of important kids and family events dominating our schedule, we have a few hobbies we enjoy, and we have a list of shows everyone's talking about at work to catch up on so we don't feel like we're missing out.

Welcome to life in the twenty-first century.

In the tiny bit of time left over, even a committed follower of Jesus can feel distant. There has never been a time in human history when being busy has been more celebrated and more messages have competed for our attention.

So what can we do about this? Do we all need to quit our jobs, drop off the radar, and become monks?

Maybe there's another option. *Maybe it's possible to feel closer to Jesus—even at work.*

If He promised to never leave us, if He promised to be with us always, then you'd have to think He would have a plan to participate in the place where most of us spend the majority of our time.

And not just for pastors—for baristas, office administrators, salespeople, teachers, stay-at-home moms, waiters, doctors, students, first responders, and every other occupation.

Life in Israel in the first century had its challenges too. In a village like Capernaum on the northwestern shore of the Sea of Galilee (non-locals called it the Lake of Gennesaret), nothing came easy.

Having enough to eat required long hours of labor, both to earn the resources and to prepare the meal. You couldn't stop and pick something up on the way home from work. You couldn't keep grinding on emails and projects after the sun went down. And you couldn't try to convince your spouse to stay up for one more episode of your latest binge-watch.

You tried to build a life for your family that was meaningful and enjoyable and that honored God and the traditions of your family. You understood you would be required to pay your taxes to Caesar and the Roman Empire, which would be collected by one of your fellow Israelites who assured you they meant well. You tried to believe them although you couldn't keep from the suspicion they were taking more than they needed in order to improve their lives.

You were probably either a peasant or a fisherman, which meant you were dependent upon factors outside of your control for your livelihood. No matter how hard you worked, you couldn't make it rain in order to grow your crops. You had to put in a full day's work whether or not the fish decided to show up.

When everything went well, life could be wonderful. But if someone you loved got sick, it almost always ended with sorrow and mourning.

You felt betrayed and disappointed by the corruption of the leaders around you who promised to help but only continued to advance their own agenda.

You dreamed of a day when you could enjoy life with God, free from the interference and wickedness of evil that felt so familiar.

It had been 400 years since God had sent a prophet. From time to time a teacher would appear to draw the people back to the promises of God's Word, but on the tough days it was hard not to feel like God had forgotten His people.

But when word started to spread about a guy named Jesus who preached the Scriptures in the synagogue with authority and healed the sick, you couldn't hold back your hope.

Maybe this Jesus was the One everyone had been waiting for.

Simon and his brother Andrew lived in this village with their family. Like many of the other fishermen in the region, they formed a partnership to lower the expensive overhead and to potentially maximize their profits. Instead of fishing on their own, they cooperated with the Zebedee family to share nets and boats.

Simon's mother-in-law was very sick, so when he saw Jesus cast an unclean spirit out of a man at the synagogue, he invited Him over to his house. We don't know if Simon went there planning to invite Jesus over or if seeing a man with a demon reminded him of his mother-in-law. I'll let you come to your own conclusion.[1]

What we do know is what happened next. Jesus shows up at the house, prays for the woman, and she's immediately healed to the point where she gets them a refreshing beverage and a snack.

At this point, Simon is definitely impressed. I love this little detail in the story: maybe his mother-in-law isn't just back to normal...maybe this is a better version of her.

[1] This is where I'd put a wink emoji or a meme if we were texting.

The whole thing goes viral and before long every sick person in the village shows up to see Jesus. It's already dark and He's tired, but He helps them all.

Flash forward a few days and we find Simon on the shore of the Sea of Galilee after a long, frustrating night of fishing.

> Luke 5:1-11, NIV
> 1 One day as Jesus was standing by the Lake of
> Gennesaret, the people were crowding around
> him and listening to the word of God. 2 He saw
> at the water's edge two boats, left there by the
> fishermen, who were washing their nets. 3 He got
> into one of the boats, the one belonging to Simon,
> and asked him to put out a little from shore. Then
> he sat down and taught the people from the boat.
> 4 When he had finished speaking, he said to
> Simon, "Put out into deep water, and let down the
> nets for a catch."
> 5 Simon answered, "Master, we've worked hard all
> night and haven't caught anything. But because
> you say so, I will let down the nets."
> 6 When they had done so, they caught such a large
> number of fish that their nets began to break. 7 So
> they signaled their partners in the other boat to
> come and help them, and they came and filled
> both boats so full that they began to sink.
> 8 When Simon Peter saw this, he fell at Jesus'
> knees and said, "Go away from me, Lord; I am
> a sinful man!" 9 For he and all his companions
> were astonished at the catch of fish they had
> taken, 10 and so were James and John, the sons of
> Zebedee, Simon's partners.

> Then Jesus said to Simon, "Don't be afraid; from now on you will fish for people." [11] So they pulled their boats up on shore, left everything and followed him.

There's so much in this passage for us to think about. As we look closer, the depth and complexity of Jesus become clearer, not just for Simon Peter but for us as well.

Jesus is preaching to a large crowd of people—that's why He got in Simon's boat. The water would've created natural amplification, allowing His words to be heard by more people.

It's safe to assume that while Simon is cleaning his nets, he's also listening to Jesus. They worked the night shift because they'd learned the fish tended to stay in deeper water to avoid the sun during the day before venturing back to the surface at night.

Their nets were large and tightly woven, which meant they were snagged and tangled with things other than fish. They had to go through the painstaking process of removing all the excess debris each night. You'd have to imagine this wasn't so frustrating when they knew they'd caught plenty of fish to make a good wage at the morning market.

But on days like this one, the process was a painful reminder that Simon had caught nothing. At least on this morning he got to hear the best teacher he'd ever heard while he was finishing his chores.

What happened next took Simon by surprise.

As Jesus finishes His message to the crowd, He turns to Simon and tells him to go back out and put out his nets again. This makes no sense. He had just finished the laborious process of cleaning his nets; if he threw them out again, he'd have to do it all over.

And what was the point? If they hadn't caught anything during the prime feeding time, why would it be better now when the fish were retreating to deeper water?

Jesus was great at preaching, He was great at healing the sick (especially a mother-in-law), He was a good enough carpenter to provide for His family—but what did He know about catching fish?

There's no doubt Simon had these thoughts. And yet, he trusted and respected Jesus enough to try it.

Immediately, and unexplainably, their nets are filled with so many fish they start to break. Broken nets would have to be repaired, so they quickly switch strategies and just dump as many fish as they can into the boats. There are so many fish the boats begin to sink.

At this point, if I were Simon I'd be so excited that I would have probably been shouting or doing a celebratory cannon ball off the back of the boat. I'd also be thinking, *This Jesus guy is a genius. I wonder what other lucrative skills He has.*

But that's not how he responds. Verse eight says that instead he behaves like Isaiah did when he saw God: "go away...leave me, Lord...I'm a sinner."

I don't think it's a coincidence that Luke decides this is the moment to change Simon's name to Simon Peter—this same understanding of the divine nature of Jesus' character is the reason the whole world remembers this disciple as Peter.

Jesus reassures him, encourages him not to be afraid, but to be certain his fishing days are over. In the moment of the greatest catch that Simon or any fisherman on the shores of Galilee had ever seen, they drop their nets without cleaning them, leave the fish there in the boat instead of taking them to the market for a massive payday, and they follow Jesus.

How did Simon explain this to his wife, to his mother-in-law, and perhaps most difficult of all, to his father? What was his brother Andrew thinking? What about their fishing partners, the Zebedee boys?

This was not a well-thought-out plan. This was not a corporate headhunter offering a new career path with superior benefits and stock options.

This was irrational. On paper, this was the worst business decision possible. This made no sense at all.

So why did all four of these guys do it? And what does it mean for us?

Any first-century fisherman would have seen this miraculous catch of fish as an inarguable sign of God's blessing. When you combine this with the teaching and the supernatural healing, they may not have understood what Jesus was up to, but there was no question in their minds that God's presence was all over Him.

Somehow that's all the convincing they needed.

When Jesus told them to follow Him, what they heard was something far more profound. It was more than "I know more about fishing than you do."

They realized that Jesus was telling them, "I know your life better than you do. And I have a purpose and a plan for you but you can't get it through carefully laid-out plans. The only way to get it is to follow Me."

Jesus extends this same invitation to every one of us.

Our path will be different from Peter's. Our roles and responsibilities won't be the same. But He offers the invitation to every person who's ever lived: "Follow Me."

He doesn't tell us exactly where we're going, and He doesn't tell us what will happen along the way. This is really difficult for us.

Most of us have trust issues with authority.

Most of us don't like to commit to something this big without a five-year plan.

Most of us think this means we'll have to become a pastor, or a missionary, and move halfway around the world.

Jesus doesn't ask us to commit to those plans—He asks us to follow Him.

It's the starting place for a genuine relationship.

Not Jesus plus a detailed account of everything that will happen to us, including details regarding who we'll marry, the names of our children, and an exhaustive account of our career trajectory.

Not Jesus at the end of an extended negotiation of offer and counter-offer.

Follow Me.

Where are we going? *Follow Me.*

What happens when we get there? *Follow Me.*

Who else is coming? *Follow Me.*

The only way to get closer to Jesus is to follow Him.

CHAPTER ONE REFLECTION QUESTIONS

What did I learn about Jesus?

What is Jesus asking me to do?

What is a practical way for me to do this?

TWO

The Greatest Sermon in History

"Seek first His Kingdom..."

You can watch my video for this chapter from the Mount of Beatitudes here: closer.milestonechurch.com

One day a long time ago someone in a marketing department had the idea to bring a little sunshine and cheery optimism to the world. They wanted to help people see their situation from a half-full perspective, so they coined the phrase "Life's a beach."

I realize lots of people love the beach—I'm married to one of these people.

While I prefer the mountains, I'll be the first to say the beach has some outstanding qualities: the soothing sounds of the shore, the refreshing water, the crash of the waves...you're probably feeling a little more relaxed as you read this paragraph.

But you have to admit the beach has its share of challenges:

> If you forget sunscreen, you'll feel the consequences for the next couple days.
>
> If a jellyfish stings you, you have to find someone to pee on you.
>
> If you're a big guy like me, you don't want to think about what happens when the inevitable grains of sand travel to undesirable areas.

On second thought, maybe that's what the creator of this slogan was trying to tell us. Even the best parts of life come with adversity. All these things happen on the same beach—*your experience depends on what you choose to focus on.*

We should not expect a frustration-free life. We should not worry or freak out over things we can't control. Instead, we should try to focus on the things we have the ability to influence and enjoy as much of life as we possibly can.

Whatever we focus on, we get full of.

When we focus on something, we seek it.

And whatever you seek, you eventually find.

I think we forget this today. Every day thousands of pieces of information pass by our sightline. What we choose to stop and focus on has a big impact on our lives.

Maybe it's just me, but it seems like everyone is outraged about something. We don't have time to keep up with all the controversies, so we rarely stop to consider whether or not they're worth our time and energy.

Our culture is addicted to outrage. Every day there's a new protest, a new target of our collective scorn, and if the whole world, or at least the people we know on social media, aren't as upset as we are, we take it as a sign the world is falling apart.

Someone is getting away with something they shouldn't and we can't calm down until they get what they deserve. This attitude knocks on all our hearts—once we open the door and let it in, we're basically committing to a life of worry, anxiety, and anger.

Remember, whatever you focus on, you get full of. If you're constantly upset about something, don't expect to have much peace when your head hits the pillow.

Now this is not naïve idealism. I'm all too familiar with the realities of evil and the genuinely upsetting injustice happening around our world. And yet, I don't think it's healthy to let that perspective consume you. Especially when your ability to influence the particular wrong is insignificant.

It's toxic in our closest relationships, but the really terrifying part is how these attitudes can overwhelm us—even with total strangers and issues that don't have an immediate impact on our daily lives.

Jesus knew how to help us focus on and seek the things that really matter. We have to push past our frustrations and the temptation to focus on the things that don't matter if we want to be close to God.

And as always, Jesus invites us to join Him in this better way of living.

He hates injustice but He rarely responds by looking for someone to blame or wasting energy on outrage. Instead, He focuses on what we can control.

Jesus understood the human proclivity toward self-righteousness even among the noblest and most well-intentioned.

All of us sons and daughters of Adam and Eve naturally follow the family tradition of excusing our own poor choices in favor of pointing the finger of blame at someone else. While it often makes us feel better for a few moments, this approach is incapable of bringing us closer to God.

Jesus has been healing the people, teaching in the synagogue, and word is starting to get out. They're intrigued and inspired by this Jesus. They want to know more. The end of Matthew 4 says that news about Him spread throughout Syria and now people are coming from Galilee, down in Jerusalem and Judea, and even the region across from the Jordan.[1]

When we read the names of these cities from a distance, they all blend together. But as I stood on the hillside and looked over the region, I realized the significance of this detail.

Galilee and Capernaum were a short walk from this spot, but the cities in Syria stretched as far as 30 miles in each direction. Jerusalem was a staggering distance—more than 106 miles away—and Judea extended even farther to the south.

When you consider that the average person could walk about 20 miles in a day during this period, you realize this

[1] "Large crowds from Galilee, the Decapolis, Jerusalem, Judea and the region across the Jordan followed him" (Matthew 4:25, NIV).

was no casual commitment. People were walking nearly a week for the opportunity to be close to Jesus.[2]

They'd been receiving ministry from Him. Now He was about to tell them what it was all about.

He goes up on a hill to take advantage of the natural amphitheater effect. There are thousands of people listening to Him and He gives His longest sermon—the most influential sermon in the history of mankind.

They named this place the Mount of Beatitudes.[3] It's in the middle of the countryside near Capernaum, and thousands of years later people come from all over the world to see it every day. How many other messages have had this kind of impact?

If you're not familiar with the Bible (and even if you are), you may not have considered who was listening to Jesus when He was preaching. Bible scholars believe there were as many as five different groups of Jewish people at any given time.

There were certain things all five groups believed—for example, they all believed the descendants of Abraham,

---

[2] To learn more about distances, walking time, and the associated dangers in the ancient world, check out Merilyn Hargis' helpful article, "On the Road" from *Christianity Today*: https://www.christianitytoday.com/history/issues/issue-59/on-road.html.

[3] Jesus starts His message with a series of statements of what it means to be blessed. That portion of the message is often called the Beatitudes. That's where the name comes from.

the people of Israel, were God's special people called to live differently than the other nations.

Whether their neighbors were Assyrian, Persian, Greek, or Roman (a successive list of world empires that enjoyed power over the Israelites), they all lived according to a different, and often hostile, worldview.

The differences between these five different groups came down to the details of whose fault it was and what they should do about it:

> The Essenes wanted nothing to do with these neighbors, so they committed themselves to live separate—even when that meant sleeping in caves.
>
> The Pharisees lived in rural areas but focused their lives on following and enforcing the complex system of laws out of their devotion to God.
>
> The Sadducees were the urban elite who ran the temple and wielded political power with the other nations.
>
> The Zealots were waiting for their moment to take up arms and violently overthrow their oppressors.

> And the common people were frustrated because they felt helpless to change their circumstances.

You may be thinking, *Jeff, is there going to be a test on all this? When are we going to talk about Jesus again? I feel farther, not closer.*

Here's why I'm taking the time to paint this picture: if you don't understand who Jesus was talking to, then you'll miss how radical His words to them were.

All five groups were frustrated.

All five groups felt beaten down and angry.

All five groups wanted to know why God hadn't come to rain down judgment upon their foes.

You may have never made the connection, but Matthew is doing everything he can to shout to his readers, "Remember the biggest moment in our history, when God's chosen prophet delivered the people from slavery, went up on a mountain to meet with God, and came back down to tell the people?"

This is like that, only a bigger deal. This Jesus? He's Moses 2.0.

Every Jew reading Matthew would have made this connection and so they would have expected plagues on Egypt, judgment on Pharaoh, and the sea swallowing the army.

There's only one problem: Jesus doesn't do any of those things.

He does the opposite. He tells the people that their real problem isn't the Romans—it's their wrong perspective and selfish attitudes. They were focused on the wrong things. They were seeking many things, but they were missing out on His Kingdom.

Jesus opens His message with a list of statements describing what it truly looks like to be blessed by God—and none of them sounds anything like what the people expected.

He then proceeds to bring their attention back to the relational requirements of the Old Testament law. In other words, when someone else wrongs you, instead of waiting for them to make it right, go another level in the love you extend to them.

Honestly, it sounds crazy. And if you're just trying to make it happen through willpower, then you're going to be miserable.

The only way you can make any progress is to get closer to Jesus. He's the only One who's ever lived this way.

That's the point.

Jesus basically says that loving and following Him aren't about living in a cave.

It's not about following complex and obscure dietary laws.

It's not about leveraging your political power to maintain ceremonial traditions.

And it's not about waiting for everyone else to receive what they deserve in order for you to do what's right.

If you want to get closer, He tells us how.

> Matthew 6:19-34, NIV
> 19 Do not store up for yourselves treasures on
> earth, where moths and vermin destroy, and
> where thieves break in and steal. 20 But store up
> for yourselves treasures in heaven, where moths
> and vermin do not destroy, and where thieves do
> not break in and steal. 21 For where your treasure
> is, there your heart will be also.
> 22 The eye is the lamp of the body. If your eyes are
> healthy, your whole body will be full of light. 23 But
> if your eyes are unhealthy, your whole body will
> be full of darkness. If then the light within you is
> darkness, how great is that darkness!

> **24** No one can serve two masters. Either you will
> hate the one and love the other, or you will be
> devoted to the one and despise the other. You
> cannot serve both God and money.
> **25** Therefore I tell you, do not worry about your life,
> what you will eat or drink; or about your body, what
> you will wear. Is not life more than food, and the
> body more than clothes? **26** Look at the birds of the
> air; they do not sow or reap or store away in barns,
> and yet your heavenly Father feeds them. Are you
> not much more valuable than they? **27** Can any one
> of you by worrying add a single hour to your life?
> **28** And why do you worry about clothes? See how
> the flowers of the field grow. They do not labor or
> spin. **29** Yet I tell you that not even Solomon in all
> his splendor was dressed like one of these. **30** If
> that is how God clothes the grass of the field,
> which is here today and tomorrow is thrown into
> the fire, will he not much more clothe you—you of
> little faith? **31** So do not worry, saying, "What shall
> we eat?" or "What shall we drink?" or "What shall
> we wear?" **32** For the pagans run after all these
> things, and your heavenly Father knows that you
> need them. **33** But seek first his kingdom and his
> righteousness, and all these things will be given
> to you as well. **34** Therefore do not worry about
> tomorrow, for tomorrow will worry about itself.
> Each day has enough trouble of its own.[4]

He tells the people that whatever you treasure will fill your heart. Whatever you look at will fill your eyes. Whatever fills your eyes fills your life.

---

[4] If you have the time, I'd encourage you to read the entire sermon, which spans Matthew 5-7.

These are powerful insights, but I love how practical Jesus makes it.

Trust Me, I know what you need. Spend less time worrying and more time focusing on what really matters. Turn your eyes to Me and My Kingdom. Prioritize Me in your life and you'll get everything else too.

Back to Moses for a moment. What was the point of the Exodus? Why did God rescue them from Egypt? Why did He part the Red Sea? Why did He give them the commandments and the tabernacle? Why did He send a pillar of cloud and fire to follow? Why did He bring them to the Promised Land?

The same reason He created the world around a perfect garden and the same reason He sent His Son: *to redeem us.*

God wants to be *with* His people. He wants to be close to us. He wants us to seek His Kingdom and, as a result, experience the life He created us to live.

You don't have to wait until all the justices in the world are worked out. You can have it right now.

The tragedy of this incredible moment is that all five groups couldn't see what was happening right in front of them. The uncreated, eternal God took on human form and became a man so He could be with His people.

They were all so worried about what everyone else was doing that they missed it.

Jesus cares more about you than flowers or birds. They don't worry about tomorrow. He cares about them and meets their needs. What will He do for you?

At the most basic level, what happens to our minds when we worry? We make our fears bigger than God.

Maybe it's the challenge in your workplace.

Maybe it's because, if you're honest, your marriage is getting worse, not better.

Maybe it's because you don't know how you ended up in this place in life and you don't know how to get out of this financial challenge, to hold it together after hearing the report from the doctor, or to make your kids behave the way you want them to.

All of these are good reasons to worry. Any of us would be tempted to obsess over these circumstances. Jesus knows that these things capture our attention and that we struggle to shake them.

Where does our heart go when we're frustrated and feel out of control? We drift farther away from God, not closer to Him.

That's why He doesn't prescribe more willpower. In another passage, He tells us to bring our burdens, the things that wear us out, the things that keep us up at night. He promises not only to take them but, in exchange, to give us His rest.[5]

When Jesus asks us to seek His Kingdom, it doesn't mean we live at the church building. It doesn't mean we spend even more time doing super-spiritual activities to earn a breakthrough.

It means we change what we focus on.

What's the treasure your heart is searching for?

What are you focused on?

What are you seeking?

Jesus is reminding us that when we treasure, focus on, and seek things other than His Kingdom, we forfeit His peace and subject ourselves to worry and fear.

He knows what we need. He wants your business, your marriage, and your kids to be healthy even more than you do. He just doesn't want those things to be more important.

---

[5] "Come to me, all you who are weary and burdened, and I will give you rest" (Matthew 11:28, NIV).

Staying close to Him won't give us control over all the factors in these areas we care so much about. But it will allow us to trust Him to do what only He can do.

CHAPTER TWO REFLECTION QUESTIONS

What did I learn about Jesus?

What is Jesus asking me to do?

What is a practical way for me to do this?

THREE

How Do You Amaze Jesus?

"I have not found such great faith even in Israel."

You can watch my video for this chapter from the synagogue in Capernaum here: closer.milestonechurch.com

It may have been a coach or a teacher. It could have been an older classmate. For more than a few, it was your first boss. And tragically for many, it was a parent.

No matter who it was, the impact is the same. It stays with you—a harsh, positional word from an authority figure:

Do as I say, not as I do.

Why? Because I said so.

Shut your mouth and do what I say.

Who do you think you are?

> Where do you get the nerve to talk to me like that?

I like to be coached. I realize I'm unusual. I've actually enjoyed a strong correction now and again during my life—and believe me, I've had more than my share. And most of them were earned.

Good leaders can be strong and humble at the same time. I believe the Bible is clear: discipline and correction are signs of love, not cruelty.

But that's not what I'm talking about. I'm referring to the other kind of poor leadership we've all experienced—it's not accurate to even call this leadership. This person has a title but no real influence, so they use their position to humiliate you, to make you feel small, essentially to turn you into a means to their own end.

They don't care about you; they only care about what you can do for them.

Unfortunately, because this attitude is fundamental to the human condition, sooner or later we all get a chance to experience it firsthand.

Jews in the first century knew all about this. They had plenty of positional leaders: religious leaders like the Pharisees and the Sadducees, the royal family of Herod, the Roman government, and even their own people who robbed them by collecting taxes for Caesar.

On a day-to-day basis, one of the biggest culprits of this behavior was the Roman soldiers. By law they could grab a Jew and force him to drop whatever he was doing to carry their heavy pack for a mile in any direction. This was inconvenient, difficult, and humiliating.[1]

As you would imagine, this created a lot of animosity in the Jewish communities. They despised the soldiers. It's also what fueled the growing community of zealots—passionate, faithful Jews who wanted to take up arms and drive these oppressors from their land.

When you understand this tension, it makes what happened in Luke 7 remarkable.

When Jesus finishes the Sermon on the Mount, He walks back down the hill into the city of Capernaum—the place that served as a ministry headquarters for Him on the north shore of the Sea of Galilee.[2]

[1] This is also what makes Jesus' teaching to carry the pack a second mile incredible. The same law permitting Romans to carry their pack a mile forbade them from going two miles because it was viewed as abusive and cruel by their superior officers. So when a Jew went the second mile, the soldier was immediately humbled because he could be punished if he was caught. He would've begged the Jew to stop. Jesus is really smart.

[2] Luke's version of the sermon is similar but considerably shorter and is sometimes called the Sermon on the Plain to distinguish it.

As He's walking through the city, He's stopped by a group of Jewish elders. They tell Jesus there's a sick servant who is about to die. This servant is highly valued by his Roman centurion master. Everything about this is unusual.

Jews didn't appeal on behalf of Roman soldiers.

Centurions don't serve their servants.

You can imagine this catches Jesus' attention.

The elders begin to plead with Jesus because they assume He shares the general contempt for Roman soldiers. They believe this situation is worthy of an exception because the man making the request loves Israel and even helped to build the local synagogue.

Jesus is intrigued, so He goes with them.

> Luke 7:1-10, NIV
> 1 When Jesus had finished saying all this to
> the people who were listening, he entered
> Capernaum. 2 There a centurion's servant, whom
> his master valued highly, was sick and about to
> die. 3 The centurion heard of Jesus and sent some
> elders of the Jews to him, asking him to come and
> heal his servant. 4 When they came to Jesus, they
> pleaded earnestly with him, "This man deserves
> to have you do this, 5 because he loves our nation
> and has built our synagogue." 6 So Jesus went with
> them.

> He was not far from the house when the centurion sent friends to say to him: "Lord, don't trouble yourself, for I do not deserve to have you come under my roof.
> 7 That is why I did not even consider myself worthy to come to you. But say the word, and my servant will be healed.
> 8 For I myself am a man under authority, with soldiers under me. I tell this one, 'Go,' and he goes; and that one, 'Come,' and he comes. I say to my servant, 'Do this,' and he does it."
> 9 When Jesus heard this, he was amazed at him, and turning to the crowd following him, he said, "I tell you, I have not found such great faith even in Israel."
> 10 Then the men who had been sent returned to the house and found the servant well.

Roman centurions were in command of between 80 and 100 soldiers. They weren't always Roman citizens, but to be entrusted with this position they would have proven their mettle in the greatest military force the world had known up to the first century. They didn't win every battle, but at their peak they conquered the entire Mediterranean region—from England and Spain through southern Europe, and including North Africa and the entire Middle East.[3]

Centurions weren't allowed to marry and have families because of the potential distraction. As a result, their servants were often more like friends and confidants than hired help. This explains why this man would be willing to ask a Jewish teacher who'd been rumored to heal people for help.

[3] That's hard to do in the board game Risk, much less in real life.

It doesn't explain his inspiring emotional intelligence and self-awareness. When you read the story, this man's character is inspiring. You might even find it *amazing*. Jesus did.

Remember, the Jewish elder said this was a man who loved Israel and helped build the synagogue. He clearly loved his servant. And he was even thinking about Jesus' needs during a great personal crisis.

When they get close to the house, he sends word to Jesus not to bother coming in the house. He said, "Lord, don't trouble yourself, for I do not deserve to have you come under my roof."

This may not seem like a big deal but it was for at least two reasons.

First, the centurion knew, understood, and respected Jewish customs and culture. If Jesus had entered the threshold, the doorway of a Gentile's home, He would have become ceremonially unclean, which would have required Him to take the time to go through cleansing. This was the trouble the centurion is referring to.

And second, when the elders come to Jesus, their big appeal to influence Jesus is that this man "deserves" to be healed. But when the man sends word to Jesus, he doesn't frame it this way. He says, "I do not deserve..." He doesn't call Jesus a teacher—he calls Him Lord.

The closer you get to Jesus, the more you know He always resists and pushes back against pride. But He loves the humble, the meek, the one who doesn't demand God's help but still asks in faith.

It's not surprising that a military commander understands authority. It is surprising that he recognizes and equates the authority of Jesus with the chain of command. Remember, this is a command-and-control, top-down, positional culture.

The rule of the Roman army was: do what your commander says or face discipline.

The rule of the Roman Empire was: do what Caesar says or die.

And this thoughtful, humble, faithful man sends word to Jesus: *Just say the word and I know my servant will be healed.*

What a radical statement. It's incredible. It doesn't make sense.

It's why we're still telling this story thousands of years later.

Jesus doesn't lay hands on the servant. Jesus doesn't even pray for him. But when they get back, the servant is healed. Jesus turns to the crowd and says, "I tell you the truth, I have not found such great faith in Israel." In other words, this guy gets it...why don't you?

When you get close to Jesus, you know how much He loves people who love others. It's a big deal to Him. I don't think He was mad at the people of Israel, but I do believe He was amazed this Roman centurion understood how different life becomes when we honor God and love and serve others.

I think sometimes we miss this too. We think getting closer to Jesus is about knowing more information or doing more spiritual things so we can deserve God's blessing in our lives.

This Roman centurion makes it so clear: *If you don't love and serve people, it's hard to be close to Jesus.*

But there was more to this man than healthy self-awareness and genuine love. He also had faith. He wasn't trying to earn God's favor, but he had no doubt that with a single word God could give him what he desired.

I hope this inspires you the way it does me. This unique combination didn't just surprise Jesus—it amazed Him. What an example he is for you and me.

Where have we allowed the thoughts of what we deserve to creep into our hearts and minds? Because the truth is, when these toxic attitudes become full-grown, we're the ones who turn into positional, top-down leaders who use people to get what we want.

It's not our goal to act this way. But we're human, so when we focus on what others owe us, it makes it impossible for us to love and serve them.

And it makes it difficult for us to come to God with genuine faith—a trust rooted in God's goodness, not in our worthiness.

Eventually most of us come to the realization that what we deserve or what we're owed is a bottomless pit we can never satisfy.

Instead, when we're considerate, when we consistently think about how we can love and serve others—not just the way we prefer to give it, but the way they receive it—we'll realize Jesus is never far away.

He cares about people. He loves them. He serves them. He completely trusts the Word of His Father. And when we do the same, we won't struggle with the sense Jesus is far away.

CHAPTER THREE REFLECTION QUESTIONS

What did I learn about Jesus?

What is Jesus asking me to do?

What is a practical way for me to do this?

FOUR

See. Believe. Worship.

"Do you believe in the Son of Man?"

You can watch my video for this chapter from the Pool of Siloam here: closer.milestonechurch.com

Some obstacles are bigger than others.

Some can be overcome or compensated for with willpower and determination.

Others can't be undone, no matter how hard you try.

It's one thing to lose your sight; it's something very different to never know the sensation of seeing.

How do you even explain that to someone?

Where would you even begin?

How would you describe colors to someone with no ability to even grasp the concept?

Research shows that less than one percent of the population is born with this condition. It also suggests that they lack the capacity for visual images—even in their dreams.

This is more serious than "I'm blind as a bat without my glasses."

This is not like getting a pair of contacts, switching from black and white to color, or upgrading from standard definition to 4k ultra-high definition.

In our world there are ongoing conversations about privilege and opportunity. We use phrases such as "No child left behind." We're concerned with giving every person the opportunity to experience the best possible version of his or her life.

But in the ancient world, nearly every culture assumed if you were born with disadvantages, then you were being divinely punished. As a result, your daily survival would depend on the mercy of others as you begged for scraps to meet your most basic needs.

Your bucket list would not be filled with exotic travel experiences, a dream home, or the ideal family. Your goals would be far lower—live to see another day.

Ninety-nine percent of us can't relate to this challenge, but we all have obstacles preventing us from being close to God.

> Maybe you feel like God doesn't hear, or doesn't even want, your prayers.
>
> Maybe you feel like you've made too many bad decisions or too many poor choices to be close to God.
>
> Maybe you feel like you don't know enough to be worthy of a relationship with Jesus.

If you've ever felt this way, and most people have, you start to lose the ability to dream of a life beyond merely surviving.

The great thing about Jesus is that He doesn't leave us there.

One day Jesus and His disciples are walking along and they see a man begging.[1] We're not sure how He knows, but Jesus makes it clear the man was born blind.

[1] This story is told in John 9. For the sake of time, I paraphrase most of it before quoting verses 35-38, but I would encourage you to read it for yourself when you get a chance.

The disciples want to know whose fault it is, so they ask Jesus whether it was the sin of the man or his parents that caused him to end up this way. Jesus rejects both options in favor of a much more inspiring reason—so this man's life can become a story that demonstrates the love and power of God.

This is the only time we know of when Jesus wiped mud on someone's eye, but it made quite the impact in this neighborhood.[2] Jesus sends the man down to the Pool of Siloam[3]—a giant reservoir that was fed by an aqueduct built during King Hezekiah's reign 700 years earlier. It was a main water source in the city of Jerusalem, but on that day it was so much more.

No one had ever seen someone that was born blind healed before and so the whole town starts freaking out. They didn't believe it was the same guy. Eventually the Pharisees show up and start questioning the man.

Instead of being excited about the supernatural, life-altering miracle this man is experiencing, the Pharisees are angry because it happened on the Sabbath. Jesus liked to perform miracles on the Sabbath because it got

[2] People used to say, "Here's mud in your eye!" as a well-meaning toast because of this story.

[3] Siloam means "sent." You could say that this is a play on words since Jesus is the one "sent by God," as the unnamed man in this story ultimately says.

everyone all stirred up.[4] It prompted this question: Did God have to play by the religious rules or did those rules only exist to serve God?

Jesus used those moments to give clear clues to anyone paying attention. He wasn't just sent on behalf of God; *He was speaking as God.*

He got the reaction He wanted.

The Pharisees interrogate this guy who is both immediately grateful and quick-witted in his verbal banter with the religious leaders. They haul in his parents too and then bring him back for more cross-examination than a *Law and Order* rerun.

They're pressuring this man to call Jesus a sinner, but he won't do it. He slows down and reiterates the facts of what happened—he was blind, now he can see.

He's not an expert in the law—he's still freaking out over shapes and colors—but even he knows that God doesn't hear the prayers of sinners. No one had ever heard of a man who was born blind gaining his sight. They didn't even know it was possible. Only God could do that.

---

[4] Jesus performed seven different miracles on the Sabbath, most notably in Matthew 12 where He called Himself the Lord of the Sabbath. The Pharisees were not amused. They wanted to kill Him for it.

This offends the Pharisees, so they kick him out. The news gets back to Jesus, so He goes looking for the guy—his eyes may have been healed, but that was only the beginning.

> John 9:35-38, NIV
> **35** Jesus heard that they had thrown him out, and when he found him, he said, "Do you believe in the Son of Man?"
> **36** "Who is he, sir?" the man asked. "Tell me so that I may believe in him."
> **37** Jesus said, "You have now seen him; in fact, he is the one speaking with you."
> **38** Then the man said, "Lord, I believe," and he worshiped him.

This is such an honest exchange, it makes me laugh. The Messiah asks this guy, "Do you believe in the Son of Man?" and he comes back with, "Who's that?" He's not being rude or short; he really doesn't know.

A blind beggar couldn't have read the Hebrew Bible on his own and he wouldn't have been allowed in the synagogue.[5] How was this man supposed to know that the Son of Man was the name of the promised Messiah as quoted in one of the most powerful and significant prophecies in the Bible?

[5] Remember the New Testament hadn't been written yet. Jesus and God-fearing people in the first century saw the Old Testament as the Bible.

It comes from Daniel 7:13, the same passage Jesus would quote when He was betrayed and questioned at the home of Caiaphas, the High Priest, only hours before He was crucified. When Jesus identified Himself as the subject of that passage, Caiaphas ripped his clothes in a theatrical, religious reaction to perceived blasphemy.

The man who could finally see didn't need all those details. He was all in on anything Jesus told him.

When Jesus basically said, "It's Me!" the man replied, "Lord, I believe" and worshiped Him. It's important for us to understand when this man said, "I believe" that he was not describing confirmation of information. This was far more relational.

The man was saying, "I'm putting all my trust in you."

Jesus could have left this man and moved on but He came back. It wasn't enough for Him to allow the beggar to physically see; He wanted to open his eyes spiritually too.

I've never met this guy but I like him. He seems like the kind of guy who would make a good friend. He had his sight back. He could've thrown Jesus under the bus so he didn't have to deal with all the Pharisees' questions, but he didn't.

He put his trust in Jesus. He said, "I believe." And then he worshiped.

What motivates someone to do this? You see Jesus for who He is, you believe, and you worship. It's the natural progression.

When you see Jesus as Lord, no one has to compel you to worship—you can't hold it in.

Do you see Jesus at work in your life?

Do you believe Jesus the way this man did—not acknowledging information but trusting Him in the context of a genuine relationship?

Have you stopped everything to worship Him?

Debates over sin won't get you closer to Jesus. Arguing over who is to blame for the challenges and problems in your life won't get you closer to Jesus.

If you want to be close to Jesus, it takes more than confirmation of information. If you want to go from being blind to gaining your sight, you have to be willing to trust—even if it means "Here's mud in your eye."

Even if it means everyone in your world starts to freak out.

Even if it means people start questioning if you are really you.

Even if they try to turn the people you love against you.

Those things aren't fun. But they're not strong enough to keep Jesus at a distance. He'll overcome every obstacle in your way.

When your eyes are open to see Him, when you believe and worship Him, then you'll always be close to Jesus.

CHAPTER FOUR REFLECTION QUESTIONS

What did I learn about Jesus?

What is Jesus asking me to do?

What is a practical way for me to do this?

Shore of Sea of Galilee

COME
AND
FOLLOW
ME

Mount of Beatitudes

S E E K
F I R S T
H I S
KINGDOM

Synagogue at Capernaum

Pool of Siloam

Boat on Sea of Galilee

Caesarea Philippi

G O

A N D

M A K E

DISCIPLES

Upper Room

Garden Tomb

FIVE

Fear and the Other Side

"Take courage. It is I. Don't be afraid."

You can watch my video for this chapter from a boat on the Sea of Galilee here: closer.milestonechurch.com

What do these things have in common: spiders, germs, clowns, flying, snakes, heights, public speaking?

I'm sure you've realized the answer.

Millions of people are scared of one or more of these things. You probably found one you immediately agreed with. Fortunately, each of these can be avoided or managed in our day-to-day lives.

For the sake of conversation, I'll tell you what I'm afraid of. In all honesty it terrifies me. It's not on the list. I don't know how many people I share it with.

My biggest fear is . . . *being hot*. I hate it.

If you're not bald, you can't appreciate how irritating it is. And if you've been to Milestone Church, you understand why our worship center often feels like a meat locker or a glorious winter's day. I told our team if they can make the A/C units snow, I'd give them a bonus.

Laughing helps us get over our fears for at least a few moments. But the scariest things come back even after we chase them away.

A random survey of Americans in 2017 produced a much different list of the top ten fears—far more common and more difficult to get over. The top fears on this list were not having enough money for the future, pollution, the cost/quality of healthcare, and corruption of government officials.[1]

I'm not sure if the people of the first century were afraid of clowns or public speaking, but besides pollution, I know they worried about the things on the second list. I'm a pastor. I work with people—these are the things that stick with them.

This is also why the people loved Jesus. He helped them overcome worry and anxiety; He healed the sick; and through His own sacrifice, He offered them a place in an eternal Kingdom.

[1] https://blogs.chapman.edu/wilkinson/2017/10/11/americas-top-fears-2017/

Fear is a powerful motivator; most psychologists believe it is *the* most powerful motivator. From my experience, a lot of marketers and media directors agree. We're constantly being targeted and manipulated by our fears.

And not only capital *F*, adrenaline-pumping, life-threatening fear. The more common fears—those revolving around our relationships, our sense of personal fulfillment, and our quality of life—constantly influence our behaviors, thoughts, and attitudes.

Every one of us makes choices every day based on fear.

Most of the things that make us really upset—the areas in which we're the most emotional—if you dig down deep enough, underneath everything else you'll find fear. This doesn't make us sick—it makes us human.

Now I'm not suggesting that all of these choices are bad. You could describe the measure of caution or the healthy respect for consequences a type of fear. These warnings protect us from situations that could hurt us. But if they constantly dominate our attention, then we won't just be afraid—*we'll be fearful.*

The challenge for us is to stay closer to Jesus than to our fears.

Jesus was no stranger to pain and discouragement. He knew what it felt like to be disrespected. He walked through dark days and challenging moments. He carried the pain of people He loved long before He went to the cross.

When Jesus taught in Capernaum around Galilee, the excited crowds were so big that He would often go out on a boat and turn around to speak back to the shore. One day He makes the 20-mile walk back to His hometown of Nazareth—a tiny village of fewer than 400 people where everyone knew each other. He taught in the synagogue—and the people were offended and unimpressed.[2]

This had to be disappointing for Mary and the rest of Jesus' family, but He was concerned because His hometown was missing out on the miracles and peace God wanted to give them.

Then word got back to Jesus that Herod Antipas had murdered His cousin, John the Baptist, because he refused to endorse Herod's adulterous relationship with his sister-in-law.[3]

Jesus had publicly said that there was no greater man than His cousin, so this news caused Him great pain.

[2] You can find the story at the end of Matthew 13.

[3] There were a lot of Herods. Antipas was the uncle of Philip the Tetrarch, who ended up marrying Salome, the dancer in the same story who asked Antipas to kill John the Baptist. Put it this way: their family was both powerful and messed up.

Whenever He felt this way, He withdrew to be with God; but this time when He tried, all the people followed Him because they wanted Him to heal the sick.

Instead of focusing on His own pain, He comforts everyone else. After He heals, He realizes they are hungry, so He tells His disciples to give them something to eat. This doesn't go over well. The disciples want to send the people off. They're annoyed; they're tired; they're worried about their stuff.

Jesus is trying to help them understand something about God, so He puts it back on them: "Give them something to eat." All they can find is a kid with a packed lunch, so they bring it to Jesus. He blesses it and it feeds 5,000 men and probably another 10-15,000 women and children.

I realize I'm giving you a lot of context, but I'm doing it for a reason. This is the set-up for one of the most iconic moments of Jesus' life. What a fascinating contrast between His inexhaustible ability to love and serve others and the disciples' inability to get over their own fear and selfishness.

There's a lesson in there for me. I'm sure there's one for you too.

After the thousands of people have been cared for, healed, fed, and sent home closer to God, Jesus finally makes His way up on a hill to spend time with His Father.

And then He sends His disciples across the Sea of Galilee for an evening boat ride.

Matthew 14:22-36, NIV
22 Immediately Jesus made the disciples get into
the boat and go on ahead of him to the other side,
while he dismissed the crowd. 23 After he had
dismissed them, he went up on a mountainside
by himself to pray. Later that night, he was there
alone, 24 and the boat was already a considerable
distance from land, buffeted by the waves
because the wind was against it.
25 Shortly before dawn Jesus went out to them,
walking on the lake. 26 When the disciples saw
him walking on the lake, they were terrified. "It's a
ghost," they said, and cried out in fear.
27 But Jesus immediately said to them: "Take
courage! It is I. Don't be afraid."
28 "Lord, if it's you," Peter replied, "tell me to come
to you on the water."
29 "Come," he said. Then Peter got down out of
the boat, walked on the water and came toward
Jesus. 30 But when he saw the wind, he was afraid
and, beginning to sink, cried out, "Lord, save me!"
31 Immediately Jesus reached out his hand and
caught him. "You of little faith," he said, "why did
you doubt?"
32 And when they climbed into the boat, the wind died
down. 33 Then those who were in the boat worshiped
him, saying, "Truly you are the Son of God."
34 When they had crossed over, they landed at
Gennesaret. 35 And when the men of that place
recognized Jesus, they sent word to all the
surrounding country. People brought all their sick
to him 36 and begged him to let the sick just touch

> the edge of his cloak, and all who touched it were healed.

The sea itself is stunning. When you look in one direction, it appears to go on forever into the horizon. But when you look the other way, your ability to view the shoreline makes it clear this is a lake.

Another feature that struck me when I went out on the very same waters was the way the hills and cliffs look down on the water. Jesus was praying, but He was also keeping an eye on His guys in the boat like you'd watch your kids at the pool.

The captain of the boat we were riding on said that the combination of warm winds from the desert side and the cooler winds coming from the north create an unusually strong weather pattern for a lake. He agreed that waves could get as high as 12 feet.

When you're on the water, you realize even if you were rowing it wouldn't take you all night to cross over—unless of course a monster storm came up out of nowhere and tossed you around. When Jesus sends them to the other side, they're headed in the direction of the Golan Heights, but the wind and the storm redirect them to the west and the region of Gennesaret.

We don't know what time they pushed off from shore, but we do know things started to get desperate in what some versions call "the fourth watch," which would have been between 3 and 6 a.m.

Weird stuff happens in those hours. It's easy to freak yourself out. You start seeing things that aren't there.

This explains their reaction to Jesus as He comes strolling on the top of the waves. They think it's a ghost. Tradition suggests there was a common belief among fishermen that if you saw a ghost walking on the water in a storm, you were going to die—kind of like a first-century Davey Jones' locker deal.

Now I've never seen Jesus walk on water, but I've put in a lot of long days in ministry. These guys are exhausted, they're frustrated, they're emotional, and they're terrified. Be honest—if you were in the boat, you would have felt the same way. That's why you have to love the disciples: they're not robots or holy superheroes—they're normal people.

Jesus leads with His go-to line in these moments: "Don't be afraid". He's not scolding them. Remember, it's like watching your kids at the pool. It's like comforting your kids when they have a bad dream and show up in the middle of the night in your bedroom.

But unlike us, Jesus doesn't wait until we go to Him; He comes looking for us.

He adds a little extra this time: "Take courage. It is I."[4] His goal is not the absence of fear. He wants the level of our courage to increase every time we get close to Him.

When you get close to Jesus, fear goes down and courage goes up.

Peter starts to feel it. His courage is powered up. He asks Jesus to call him out onto the water, and the next thing anyone knows he's actually doing it. If ever there was a moment worth putting on Instagram, this was it.

As long as Peter keeps his eyes on Jesus, he keeps taking steps. The moment he's distracted by the wind and the waves, he starts to sink.

This goes way beyond pre-dawn storm walks on water—all of life works this way.

Peter prays a great prayer I recommend you memorize: "Lord, save me!" When Jesus responded by asking Peter why he doubted, I don't think Jesus is correcting Peter—I think He's encouraging him.

---

[4] Bible scholars suggest this little phrase, "It is I," can easily be translated as a clear derivative to God's declaration to Moses, "I Am," where we get God's holiest name, *Yahweh* (technically *YHWH*), and where we get the word "Jehovah." This would make this encounter another clue to the authentic identity of Jesus we'll talk about in chapter 6.

It's way more "You were so close! You almost had it. Why didn't you keep going?" than "If you were more spiritual, disciplined, and mature, this wouldn't have happened."

Jesus pulls Peter in and gets in the boat and everything goes still. They all worship Him. Although it's been terrifying and difficult, they're all closer to Jesus after this night. They're convinced He's more than a teacher.

Probably at this point the guys all remembered their other stormy night on the water when they thought they were going to die while Jesus was sleeping. Don't be too hard on them—they were freaked out.

We all tend to miss things when we're emotional. Have you ever lost your phone and started to panic only to discover it was in your pocket—or even in your other hand—all along? I'm glad I'm not the only one. Let's give these guys a little grace.

When they finally reach the shore, they go right into more ministry. They haven't slept, they've been through a traumatic experience, but the Bible doesn't mention any frustration or complaining.

It's amazing how things change when we get close to Him.

What does it look like for us to stay closer to Jesus than to our fear?

> Does it mean we don't have bad days?
>
> Does it mean we never get afraid?
>
> Does it mean we don't get frustrated, act selfishly, and complain?

I doubt it.

But when you're close to Jesus, you also know how to take courage in the middle of the storm. This is pretty simple—look to Jesus instead of your fear.

Don't hear what I'm not saying. The closer you get to Jesus, your opportunities to struggle with fear go up, not down. He sends anyone who follows Him ahead to the other side.

To the other side of the office.

To the other side of the neighborhood.

To the other side of the world.

To the other side of the kitchen table.

He's always sending those who love Him to those who are hurting. He won't send you to everyone, but He will send you to someone. And when He does, it's never convenient. It's never easy. There's always fear involved.

As you're reading these words, you may already know the other side He's sending you to. And if you have a pulse, you're uncertain. You're a little afraid. It's okay. If you stay close to Him, your courage will go up and eventually your fear will go down.

We never outgrow being sent to the other side. The sooner you realize this, the less you'll wrestle with frustration and fear. And you'll find a greater ability to keep your eyes on Him.

CHAPTER FIVE REFLECTION QUESTIONS

What did I learn about Jesus?

What is Jesus asking me to do?

What is a practical way for me to do this?

SIX

The Question that Demands an Answer

"Who do you say I am?"

You can watch my video for this chapter from the Gates of Hell at Caesarea Philippi here: closer.milestonechurch.com

When was the last time you were asked a question?[1]

Questions are a constant part of life. No one knows this better than moms of small children. They face hundreds of questions before nap time.

Answering questions can be difficult—but it's not as hard as it used to be. If you enjoy the basic technological advances available today, then you can ask Siri, Alexa, Google, or Wikipedia as many times as you need to.

[1] You may be thinking, *Right now. That was a question.* Congratulations! You figured it out.

As amazing as these devices are, they can't give us all the answers we need.

Some questions are not important: Have you seen that video on YouTube?

Some questions feel too significant to answer quickly: What's the most important thing you've ever learned?

Some questions may not have an answer: How come "I could care less" and "I could *not* care less" mean the same thing?

Some questions we want to answer yes but we feel like we should say no: Do you want fries with that?

We all realize some questions are more important than others. There's a huge difference between "Can you pass the salt?" and "Will you marry me?"

Jesus has one of those big, life-altering questions for every person who's ever lived. None of us can avoid it. None of us can answer for someone else.

But for those of us who want to get closer to Jesus, we have to wrestle with this question. He may ask it more than once, but make no mistake, this is a question He's going to ask you.

The first time He asked the question to His disciples was a fascinating story under unusual circumstances. In fact, the occasion became one of the most important moments of Jesus' ministry.

One day Jesus is walking with the disciples and they make their way up the region of Caesarea Philippi, about 40 miles north of the shores of the Sea of Galilee at the base of Mount Hermon. This sounds fairly normal to us but it would have freaked the disciples out.

You see, this was a place good Jewish boys didn't go. It was lush, green, and beautiful because it was an area fed with some of the headwaters of the Jordan River. This made the region popular with rulers like Augustus Caesar, who gave the land to Herod Philip.[2] To honor this gesture, Philip built temples on the site and changed the name to Caesarea Philippi in honor of both of them.

Prior to that time the site was called *Paneas* after Pan, the Greek god of the forest. This was an agricultural region where the people depended on the land to produce their livelihood. Because they believed Pan was a fertility god, they thought he would go in the ground at the end of harvest until he returned the next spring.

[2] Another of Herod the Great's sons, often called Philip the Tetrarch or Herod VI. His wife was a dancer named Salome who asked for John the Baptist's head in a basket as a gift.

To earn his favor, one of the despicable things they would do was offer human sacrifice in the back of a cave where the spring that fed the area was located. There were places in the cave where the rocks separated, causing heat and steam to come up out of the earth. Because of this apparent doorway to the underworld, the place was also called the Gates of Hell.

According to tradition, if the blood from the sacrifice stayed in the cave, the offering was received and the land would yield a great harvest. If the blood was carried down to the waters below the cave, it meant the sacrifice had been rejected.

Pan is sometimes depicted as a half-human, half-goat creature, so many scholars believe that the festivals would include lewd, ritualistic sexual immorality.

You're probably starting to understand why Jews saw this place as off limits.

But it's also telling that Jesus chose this place—claimed by the three great ruling kingdoms of this area—as the location to ask the disciples this pointed question: "Who do people say I am?"[3]

This is not the big question—but it sets the stage for it.

---

[3] This beautiful location is claimed by the Greek god Pan, Caesar Augustus, and Philip.

Matthew 16:13-20, ESV
13 Now when Jesus came into the district of
Caesarea Philippi, he asked his disciples, "Who do
people say that the Son of Man is?" **14** And they said,
"Some say John the Baptist, others say Elijah, and
others Jeremiah or one of the prophets." **15** He said
to them, "But who do you say that I am?" **16** Simon
Peter replied, "You are the Christ, the Son of the
living God." **17** And Jesus answered him, "Blessed
are you, Simon Bar-Jonah! For flesh and blood has
not revealed this to you, but my Father who is in
heaven. **18** And I tell you, you are Peter, and on this
rock I will build my church, and the gates of hell
shall not prevail against it. **19** I will give you the
keys of the kingdom of heaven, and whatever
you bind on earth shall be bound in heaven, and
whatever you loose on earth shall be loosed in
heaven." **20** Then he strictly charged the disciples
to tell no one that he was the Christ.

The disciples were usually two steps behind Jesus, so you get the sense they're reaching for the answers they think Jesus wants to hear. They probably did that thing most people do when we're not sure about our answer—our voice goes up at the end until our answer trails off: *Elijah? Jeremiah? One of the prophets?*

Now the time has come. The warm-up is over.[4] He turns to them and asks, "But what about you? Who do *you* say I am?"

[4] As Nacho Libre would say, "Let's get down to the nitty gritty." He's quite the theologian.

Our man Peter was not perfect. He made his share of mistakes. But this was a shining moment for him. He stepped right up and crushed it: You are the Messiah, the Son of the living God.

How did he do it? How did he know? Did he put together all the pieces of the puzzle using information and evidence? Did someone slip him the answer? Was it a lucky guess?

Jesus makes it clear.

It wasn't information. It wasn't a compelling presentation or a persuasive sales job. Peter understood because God revealed Jesus to him. He'd seen glimpses of Jesus, but now it all came together.

Based on this revelation, Jesus blesses him and makes three big statements: First, his name goes from Simon (reed blown by the wind) to Peter (rock). Second, Jesus promises to build His Church on the rock of this revelation. It's His Church, not Peter's, and it will never end. And third, the Gates of Hell—unimaginable wickedness like the kind happening in the cave behind Him—couldn't overcome it.

That's why Jesus brought the disciples to this place to ask them the question.

He wants them to see what He cares about. He wants them to know what He's doing can't be stopped. He wants them to know the one thing He promised to build was His Church.

His plans haven't changed. He is who He says He is. He's going to accomplish His purpose through His Church. And He's inviting us to join Him. He wants us to be close.

Information won't get you there. Having a genuine revelation of Jesus will.

Whether or not you want to be close to Him, you still have to answer the question: *Who is Jesus?*

There are a lot of options. Many people think He was a great moral teacher. Others think He was a prophet. A few even believe He's a fictional character—that He never even existed.

You probably realize that, like Peter, I believe Jesus is the Messiah, the Son of the living God. He's fully God and fully man. Every once in a while someone musters up the courage to ask me if I ever doubt or if I wonder if Jesus wasn't who He said He was. I appreciate their honesty—I'd rather have them tell me where they are, not where they think I want them to be.

I believe the credibility of the historical accounts of Jesus hold up to rigorous scrutiny. Jewish and Roman historians detail His life, death, and influence on the first century. I also believe He was more than a prophet and a teacher. He claimed the authority to forgive sin, He received worship, and He identified Himself with God's most sacred name, *YHWH*, or in a simple translation, "*I Am.*"

These concepts satisfy my intellectual curiosity and they help me know about Jesus; but it's not how I know Him. I know Him because, just like Peter, God revealed Him to me.

Do you have a revelation of Jesus?

Now you're probably thinking, *Jeff, how does that happen? Does God just drop it out of the sky? How does it work? Does God come to us or do we go to Him?* The answer is yes.

The Bible says we love Him because He first loved us, but it also says we'll find God when we seek Him with all our heart.[5]

You don't have to wonder if God's reaching out to you—like a great Father, He always knows where we are. He gave us His Word, He speaks to us through our circumstances, and He draws near when we gather in corporate worship.

[5] "We love because he first loved us" (1 John 4:19, NIV); "You will seek me and find me when you seek me with all your heart" (Jeremiah 29:13, NIV).

Jesus wants us to be confident in our ability to hear His voice. He wants us to know He's promised to build His Church. And He wants us to remember He has a place for us in His plan.

Because of these we can stay close to Jesus, even at the "Gates of Hell."[6]

[6] Most people have heard this phrase as a metaphorical image instead of a physical description. While it may be both, there is no doubt Jesus was thinking of the cave He was standing in front of.

CHAPTER SIX REFLECTION QUESTIONS

What did I learn about Jesus?

What is Jesus asking me to do?

What is a practical way for me to do this?

SEVEN

Servant King, Risen Lord

"He is not here; He has risen, just as He said."

You can watch my video for this chapter from the Garden of Gethsemane and the Garden Tomb here: closer.milestonechurch.com

The week leading up to Easter is often called the Passion week.[1] It begins with the Triumphal Entry (Palm Sunday) and then culminates the following Sunday with Easter.

When Jesus and His disciples made their way up to Jerusalem for the actual Easter Sunday, they were joining the crowds of people heading there to celebrate the Passover.[2] The Bible makes it clear the streets were crowded. There were festivals and events all over, and the city was buzzing with energy and excitement.

---

[1] "Passion" comes from the Latin word "to suffer."

[2] No matter which direction you're coming from, Jews always say you go up to Jerusalem. It's literally a city on a hill. You realize how significant this concept is when you're there.

As I moved through this same ancient city and walked on many of these same streets, I could relate. When you look at the maps in the back of the Bible or in a commentary, you can't get the sense of how close together everything is.

I went from the Garden of Gethsemane at the base of the Mount of Olives over to the Garden Tomb on a Friday evening. There were tens of thousands of pilgrims making their way through the city for evening prayers, while everyone else was making final preparations for the weekly Sabbath dinner with their family. Traffic was terrible, streets were jammed, there was strong military and police presence, and you could feel the tension in the air.

On one hand it was overwhelming, yet at the same time, it gave me a strong sense of how Jerusalem might have felt all those years ago.

It made me feel closer to Jesus.

At the risk of stating the obvious, the last week of Jesus' life was a big deal. Honestly, without that week, you and I could not be close to God.

You may have never thought about this but the Gospel of John is 21 chapters long—the first 12 chapters cover approximately 3 years of Jesus' ministry while the last 9 take place during this one week.

John, like the rest of the Gospel writers, wants to make sure we understand how critical this was. Jesus Himself continually described it as the reason He came.

On Thursday night the disciples celebrate the faithfulness of God through the Passover meal. Unless you come from a Jewish family, you probably think of this moment as the Last Supper. The Passover is a reminder of when God's people were captive in Egypt under Pharaoh and the Lord told them to take the blood of a spotless lamb and paint it over their doorpost. When the angel of death moved through the land and saw the blood over the doorpost, it would pass over their home and spare their firstborn.

The life of the lamb was given in exchange for the life of their firstborn son. This tenth and final plague was so devastating, the king of Egypt finally relented and let the Israelites go to return to their homeland. God parted the Red Sea so His people could make their exodus from bondage into glorious freedom.

They celebrated so they would not forget what God had done for them.

God never forgot, but He knew what they didn't. The Passover was a prophetic picture of a day when the perfect lamb of God would give His life for the sins, not just of Israel, but the whole world. But this time, death would not pass over the firstborn Son of God—He would take it on Himself so He could lead all those who believe in Him from bondage to an eternal freedom.

Don't feel bad if you never realized this before. The disciples didn't get it either. They didn't connect the dots in order to understand what was happening.

Jesus tells them He's going away to prepare a place for them, and as you'd imagine, they're crushed by this idea.

He makes several comforting promises, including the commitment to send the Comforter, the Holy Spirit, to be with them. He confronts Judas and reveals him as the betrayer, inspires the rest of them to true servant leadership, implores them to love and serve one another, prays for them, and finishes the meal.

By this time Jesus is feeling the pressure to a degree we can't comprehend. He loved Judas and He was grieved by his choice. He knew the disciples, His natural family, and His followers were all about to face pain, sorrow, and even shame beyond anything they'd experienced. And He was feeling the weight of what was about to happen.

So Jesus did what He always did in those moments—He withdrew in prayer to be with His Father.

The Garden of Gethsemane is at the base of the Mount of Olives. The word literally means "oil press," which made it the perfect place to pray when feeling indescribable pressure—a pressure so intense it could make someone sweat blood.[3]

The garden, which is probably more accurately described as an olive tree orchard, is still there today, complete with some 1,500-year-old olive trees.

He's giving us another clue, another insight into how life is supposed to work. When we feel pressure and pain, our tendency is often to move farther away from God. Jesus shows us those are the moments to focus on prayer and worship so we can move closer to Him.

> Matthew 26:36-46, NIV
> **36** Then Jesus went with his disciples to a place
> called Gethsemane, and he said to them, "Sit here
> while I go over there and pray." **37** He took Peter
> and the two sons of Zebedee along with him, and
> he began to be sorrowful and troubled.**38** Then
> he said to them, "My soul is overwhelmed with
> sorrow to the point of death. Stay here and keep
> watch with me."
> **39** Going a little farther, he fell with his face to the
> ground and prayed, "My Father, if it is possible,
> may this cup be taken from me. Yet not as I will,
> but as you will."

---

[3] "And being in anguish, he prayed more earnestly, and his sweat was like drops of blood falling to the ground" (Luke 22:44, NIV); the medical condition is known as hematidrosis, the rupturing of a capillary due to extreme stress, resulting in blood coming through the skin.

> 40 Then he returned to his disciples and found
> them sleeping. "Couldn't you men keep watch with
> me for one hour?" he asked Peter. 41 "Watch and
> pray so that you will not fall into temptation. The
> spirit is willing, but the flesh is weak."
> 42 He went away a second time and prayed, "My
> Father, if it is not possible for this cup to be taken
> away unless I drink it, may your will be done."
> 43 When he came back, he again found them
> sleeping, because their eyes were heavy. 44 So he
> left them and went away once more and prayed
> the third time, saying the same thing.
> 45 Then he returned to the disciples and said to
> them, "Are you still sleeping and resting? Look, the
> hour has come, and the Son of Man is delivered
> into the hands of sinners. 46 Rise! Let us go! Here
> comes my betrayer!"

One of the things I never realized before was the number of tombs and graves all over the Mount of Olives. This explains why, when Jesus goes to the garden, He knows Caiaphas the High Priest, the Sanhedrin, and the religious leaders would not come to get Him—because being in a graveyard would make them unclean.

When Judas comes for Jesus, he brings a mob fit for capturing a criminal, not someone claiming to be the Son of God. Caiaphas had wanted to kill Jesus for quite some time but he couldn't get Him in the garden and he couldn't deliver a death sentence. Only the Romans could do that, but they'd been working on it and the wheels were in motion.

Nazareth wasn't the only time Jesus was rejected by His own people. It pained Jesus to realize that His own people couldn't see Him for who He really was. They were all expecting the Messiah to be a powerful king who defeated all the kingdoms of the earth. And make no mistake, Jesus is and did, but not in the way they wanted or expected.

They had no concept for a Messiah, a King, who came in the form of a servant. They'd never heard of such a thing, even though it's right there waiting for them in Isaiah 53.

So when He came, in the moment for which they'd waited expectantly for thousands of years, they missed Him. When God came near, they remained far away. There's a lesson in there for us.

As Jesus is wrestling with the pressure in the garden, He asks His closest followers to stand and pray with Him. They talk a big game but they end up sleeping. And instead of rebuking them, He extends them grace and understanding.[4]

One last thought about this unforgettable scene: Sometimes as a young preacher I would appeal to people by saying that when Jesus went to the cross He was

[4] In a few weeks when they were the ones being beaten, thrown in jail, and leading the people in the book of Acts, they didn't sleep then. They were "devoted" to prayer.

thinking about us. It's good preaching, but it's not what the Bible says.

Think about this: Jesus said that He could have called down a legion of angels to save Himself from the cross. He said that no one took His life from Him, but He gave it willingly. Under the stress and pressure that only the sins of all humanity could produce, Jesus appealed to His Father and asked Him if there was any other way.

Here's why this is so significant: This story goes all the way back to Genesis 3 and the first two people. They were in a garden with God without sin. You can't get any closer. But one day they decide to put their own will above God's. This creates a separation from God that has been passed down in the nature of every human being.

The problem started in a garden. Where do you go to solve that problem? Back to a garden.

How do you solve it? Instead of choosing your own selfish desires, you pray, "Not my will but Yours."

That prayer always brings you closer to God.

Judas and his mob show up in the garden and they drag Jesus off to the home of Caiaphas the High Priest. The religious leaders motivate people to lie as false witnesses, hoping they'll be able to find a reason to bring charges against Him that are serious enough to motivate the Romans to kill Him.

It doesn't work. Even with a bunch of liars doing their best to indict Him with phony charges, they can't do it. Finally, Jesus connects Himself to the Messianic Kingdom from Daniel 7 and again identifies Himself as "I Am."[5] Each of these statements is the equivalent of claiming to be God—the High Priest tears his garments and arrests Jesus.

Jesus did a lot of walking. He would have seen firsthand the Roman practice of crucifixion. The purpose was to humiliate and intimidate any other potential troublemaker with a clear understanding of how Rome enforced the Pax Romana.[6] He likely spent the rest of the night remembering and agonizing over the times He'd walk by a criminal dying on a cross.

---

[5] The scene takes place in Matthew 26:62-64: "Then the high priest stood up and said to Jesus, 'Are you not going to answer? What is this testimony that these men are bringing against you?' But Jesus remained silent. The high priest said to him, 'I charge you under oath by the living God: Tell us if you are the Messiah, the Son of God.' 'You have said so,' Jesus replied. 'But I say to all of you: From now on you will see the Son of Man sitting at the right hand of the Mighty One and coming on the clouds of heaven'" (NIV); the passage Jesus quotes is Daniel 7:13: "In my vision at night I looked, and there before me was one like a son of man, coming with the clouds of heaven. He approached the Ancient of Days and was led into his presence" (NIV).

[6] Latin for "the peace of Rome." They believed this was their gift to the world through their form of civilization, including roads, military power, and localized government. Crucifixion was a last resort, a form of punishment so severe, Roman citizens were not eligible for it.

In the morning they bring Him to Pilate, who's looking for a reason to let Jesus go but is unwilling to upset the Jews. Jesus is severely beaten, humiliated, forced to carry His own cross, and led to His death.

We can't get our minds around how dark this day must have been. And not just as a spiritual metaphor—the sun actually went black. For anyone who loved Jesus, all hope was lost. There was nothing left.

On Saturday Pilate and the Pharisees are concerned the followers will steal the body and deceive everyone, so they fortify the tomb with Roman soldiers and seal it. If the seal was broken, the Roman soldiers would face the penalty of death. Without any military presence, a burial stone would have required ten or more men to move.

> Matthew 28:1-6a, NIV
> 1 After the Sabbath, at dawn on the first day of the
> week, Mary Magdalene and the other Mary went to
> look at the tomb.
> 2 There was a violent earthquake, for an angel of
> the Lord came down from heaven and, going to
> the tomb, rolled back the stone and sat on it. 3 His
> appearance was like lightning, and his clothes
> were white as snow. 4 The guards were so afraid of
> him that they shook and became like dead men.
> 5 The angel said to the women, "Do not be
> afraid, for I know that you are looking for Jesus,
> who was crucified. 6 He is not here; he has risen,
> just as he said."

When it looked like all hope was lost, when it looked like death had the final say, history was forever changed. The women go to the tomb, there's an earthquake, and an angel shows up to tell them Jesus is not there.

They run to tell the disciples and they run right into Jesus, who tells them to meet Him in Galilee.

There's something incredible and powerful about the Garden Tomb. It's right in the middle of the city. You step down a side street and into a doorway and you're whisked away. We don't even know for certain if this is exactly where this was.

We don't worship an empty hole or a physical location.

We worship the Jesus who got up out of the grave.

There's no mystery to that part—we know for certain.

The only reason any of us can get close to God is because of what happened in that tomb.

Through the cross and the empty tomb, Jesus tells us, "I have defeated death, sin, and the powers of darkness in order to give you new life and a place with Me forever."

Jesus didn't come to give self-help principles to people with problems.

Jesus didn't come to give self-righteous people a little extra help to be good enough.

Jesus didn't come to make bad people better, or bad people good.

Jesus came to bring dead people back to life.

This moment changed human history—it can change your life too.

CHAPTER SEVEN REFLECTION QUESTIONS

What did I learn about Jesus?

What is Jesus asking me to do?

What is a practical way for me to do this?

EIGHT

Close to the Purpose, Close to the Person

"Go and make disciples..."

You can watch my video for this chapter from the Upper Room here: closer.milestonechurch.com

Daniel Kahneman is an expert in the science of the psychology of judgment and decision-making (often referred to as behavioral economics). His work has been exceptional enough for him to have received the Nobel Prize in Economic Sciences back in 2002.[1]

One of his biggest contributions is known as Peak-End Theory, which can be summarized as the human

[1] You may have heard about the book he wrote, *Thinking Fast and Slow*, or the best-selling book Michael Lewis wrote about his work, called *The Undoing Project*. Both books are complex but filled with fascinating insights. They're also the kind of books you buy and leave on your desk if you want to impress your friends/co-workers.

propensity to remember and be influenced by the most intense moment and the last moment in an experience. You carry those with you and they shape how you interact with the world.

Here are just a few examples of how this impacts us:

> If you go on a vacation, your experience is shaped by the best/worst moment and the last moment. This influences whether or not you go back—and if you see the cost as a worthwhile investment or a total waste of money.
>
> Your opinion of your college years is largely shaped by the best/worst moments and how things ended. Later, when your school calls and asks you for money—and they will—this will probably determine your generosity level.
>
> Your perception of your marriage is mostly influenced by the best/worst moments *and* your last interaction. In other words, the vacation of a lifetime can give you the misguided sense that everything is wonderful, while a fight today over-inflates the feeling that things are headed for trouble.

What's really interesting to me is when the best/worst moments are also the last interaction. I've only recently started thinking about this, but there's no doubt this is the exact scenario the disciples went through at the end of the Gospels.

We can't relate to the emotions they experienced in those last few days.

Their friend, their teacher, their Lord was betrayed by one of their own. They'd left everything to follow Him. Their future, their hopes, their entire lives were caught up in Him. Now it was all gone. He was arrested like a criminal, humiliated, beaten so viciously He was unrecognizable.

Then He faced the indignity of being stripped naked, nailed to a tree, and planted under the elements in a place of high visibility as a warning to any who followed Him.

This would be traumatic and haunting to witness if the person was a total stranger. Try to imagine how this feels when it's the person you love the most.

And yet, from the depths of this level of despair, He did what He promised. He didn't stay dead. Death couldn't hold Him. Caiaphas' plan had failed. Pilate's soldiers couldn't keep the seal intact; they couldn't stop the stone from being rolled away.

Now try to imagine the joy and elation they felt when they were reunited with Jesus. It's one thing to command the wind and the waves. It's something totally different to overcome the power of death.

This isn't just one of the world's most famous stories—it actually happened, in real time, to real people who experienced the full range of emotions.

Jesus isn't a ghost. He walks with disciples on the road to Emmaus and explains the Scriptures to them. He walks into the room and let's them touch His hands and side. He goes back to the shores of Galilee to find Peter, James, and John the way He first called them—and they eat breakfast together.

By the way, don't miss the significance of this. I won't speak for you, but let me go firmly on the record to acknowledge my joy in knowing that our glorified bodies will be able to eat delicious food!

They go from the shores of the Sea of Galilee to a nearby mountain, where the rest of the disciples join them. I love the detail in this part of the story: "When they saw Him, they worshiped Him; but some doubted."[2] Really? This wasn't enough for them? What more does Jesus need to do to convince them?

Let's be honest—this whole ordeal is a lot to handle. They've got to be delirious at some level. And before

[2] "When they saw him, they worshiped him; but some doubted" (Matthew 28:17).

we're too quick to criticize them, we have to admit that we've been known to do the same thing when God shows up in our lives.

It's another helpful reminder—getting closer to Him is not about getting more information or even seeing Him do the miraculous. Most of us think those are the missing pieces we need. The truth is the same for us as it was for them.

Getting closer to Jesus is about trusting His Word and looking for His hand at work in our lives right in the middle of our painful circumstances.

Stories of these appearances have been spreading around the world from that first Easter Sunday. The Bible says, in addition to the ones I've listed, He also appeared to more than 500 of His followers at the same time. As you might imagine, you couldn't keep these stories quiet. They were spreading all throughout the region.

In fact, the message of these stories hasn't stopped since—making it's way around the world and into nearly every language known to man.

Unfortunately, in all the excitement, too often the critical importance of the last thing Jesus said has been forgotten.

In Luke 24, Jesus tells His disciples that He's going to send them what His Father has promised. He explains this further by telling them to stay in the city until the Holy Spirit comes and fills them with power.

Of course this would happen just like Jesus promised.

Luke picks up the story in Acts 1 by repeating the promise Jesus gives them and adding that this power will give them the ability to be His witnesses in Jerusalem, Judea, Samaria, and the ends of the earth. We'll come back to this in a moment.

After Jesus ascends to heaven, the disciples head back into the city just as He told them to. While they're waiting for the promise, they devote themselves to prayer. They consider two men to replace Judas and decide on Matthias.

Around this time the celebration of Pentecost takes place.[3] While the disciples are gathered in an upper room, they're filled with the Holy Spirit, they speak in other tongues as the Spirit enables them, and a group of traveling pilgrims are amazed to recognize their unique languages.

Finally, the moment they'd been waiting for comes. I don't think it's a coincidence that the disciples could see from

[3] "Pentecost" is from the Latin for "50 days later," a Jewish festival following Passover.

the roof of this building the Mount of Olives where Jesus gave them their final instructions.

This promised power quickly becomes evident as Peter finds a new boldness, preaches the first sermon in the history of the Church, and thousands repent and follow Christ. These followers commit themselves to prayer and teaching and to serve one another; supernatural signs and wonders become a part of their daily lives; and, as you might imagine, people were being added every day.

Now back to the last thing Jesus told them. It was the setup for this explosive start of the Church.

Back in Luke 24, Jesus led them out of Jerusalem to the vicinity of Bethany, a small village on the southern slope of the Mount of Olives where He blessed them and ascended into heaven. Matthew gives us the details of what He told them before He left them.[4]

> Matthew 28:18-20, NIV
> **18** Then Jesus came to them and said, "All authority in heaven and on earth has been given

[4] If you're confused or bothered by the chronology of these events, I want to help you. First, you have to remember we think far more linearly than people did in the first century. This wouldn't have bothered them. Second, there's still enough room in the narrative to piece these accounts together. For example, Matthew tells us that the disciples went to a mountain in Galilee in verse 16, but in verse 17 he paints a picture of an interaction with Jesus, before adding, "Then Jesus came to them..." even though He was already with them at that point. It's not a stretch to suggest that this describes the encounter on the Mount of Olives that Luke alludes to since both the chapel and Church of the Ascension are located on the Mount of Olives.

> to me. 19 Therefore go and make disciples of all nations, baptizing them in the name of the Father and of the Son and of the Holy Spirit, 20 and teaching them to obey everything I have commanded you. And surely I am with you always, to the very end of the age."

These are Jesus' final words to His closest friends and followers. These are His parting instructions. This is Matthew's version of what Luke describes as being a witness.[5]

Jesus commissions and authorizes His followers with all the authority in heaven and on Earth entrusted to Him by His Father. He sends them to go and make disciples of all the "nations." The Greek word is *ethnos*, and it may be more precise to think of this as "ethnicities," or "people groups," than as political nation states.

But what I really want to focus on is this idea: "make disciples." This is the goal, the target, the final, definitive word from Jesus. He didn't tell us to have conferences and get more information. Those things can be valuable, but they're not the goal. The goal is to make a disciple.

And here's the critical point: disciples have to be made. They don't make themselves.

---

[5] You may recognize this passage as the Great Commission. Bible scholars aren't certain who originated this term, but most believe it grew in popularity through the efforts of Hudson Taylor.

How do you know if someone is a disciple? They learn to obey everything Jesus told them—which includes making disciples!

If this sounds a little daunting or intimidating, it's because it is. You may be thinking, *Jeff, this is for the special people. This is for pastors like you who God calls and sends uniquely.* Two thoughts may be helpful here.

First, the tense of the verb "go" here is literally "as you're going." Why would I mention this? Because I think the inference is that this is not a special one-time trip. This isn't "Go now and make a disciple." It's better understood as "Wherever you go, make disciples."

And second, Jesus promises to always be with us, even to the very end. This is great news. I can't help but think back to Matthew 16 when He promised to build His Church. He empowers us to lead, but He promises to provide the power. We're not doing this on our own.

Remember the concept from the start of the chapter, peak-end theory? I think it can help us. When we think of our Christian experience, we evaluate it by the best/worst moments and our last experience.

If you take these words from Jesus seriously, you realize that He's empowered and invited you to join Him in His mission. Your opinion of what it's like to follow Jesus will be shaped by both the greatest challenges and the highest moments of joy. But if all of these moments are decades behind us, we can't help but feel distant and disconnected from Jesus.

To state it more simply, if you want to be close to His person, you have to stay close to His purpose.

The farther we drift away from His clear purpose to make disciples, the more difficult it will be to feel close to Him.

Does this mean that making disciples and prioritizing His purpose will be easy? No way. In fact, you can be sure it will include painful moments, serious adversity, and more than a few days when everything in you wants to give up.

But the one thing it won't be is boring. You won't be left to wonder if Jesus cares about what you spend your days thinking about.

In those moments, we're reminded that it's not up to us or our own strength and power to get the job done. We can't change anyone—only God's Spirit can do that. Peter and the rest of the disciples realized this by the end of the book of Acts.

Jesus never asked us to do it this way. He promised His power and His presence to anyone, from anywhere, with any background, of any age, willing to join His purpose.

CHAPTER EIGHT REFLECTION QUESTIONS

What did I learn about Jesus?

What is Jesus asking me to do?

What is a practical way for me to do this?

Conclusion

You made it to the end of this journey. Now the question becomes, where do we go from here?

When you're close to Jesus, you realize this is a question we keep asking throughout the course of our lives. We commit our allegiance, our hearts, our lives to Him one time like a wedding vow—He doesn't keep checking on us to see if He's still Lord. He's not unclear about His identity, but He waits for us to receive Him for who He truly is.

We can't earn our way into a relationship with Jesus. The Bible makes it clear He made a way for us when we were hostile, strangers, unfaithful, disobedient—without hope and without God in the world.

This sounds discouraging if you're still impressed with yourself. But once you become aware of the extent of your limitations, this becomes the best news you've ever heard.

It doesn't matter who your parents were; it doesn't matter how you were raised; it doesn't matter how much of the Bible you know. What matters is whether or not you acknowledge your need for God and repent. I realize this is a loaded word.

At the most basic level, repent means "to change your mind." The root comes from the same concept as the military notion of marching in one direction, stopping, turning 180 degrees, and then resuming in this new direction.

We repent from sin to righteousness in Christ.

We repent from trusting in our own strength to receiving His.

We repent from trying to be god to loving and obeying the one true God.

We repent from worshiping money, our career, our family, and even our ministry to worshiping God.

God doesn't receive us into His family on the basis of our righteousness. We can't do enough spiritual activity to make ourselves perfect. As long as we're flawed, we can't be welcomed into God's presence—because while God is love, He's also holy.

Learning spiritual information may be helpful, but it doesn't make us a Christian. Only choosing to put your trust in Jesus to make you right with God can do that.

This is not a light-hearted, flippant decision. The military metaphors are appropriate. One time Jesus compared surrendering our lives to Him like a king who gathered his armies and decided whether or not to send them to war or to surrender in peace.

While sobering, this illustration is accurate. But it's not comprehensive.

Perhaps the most well-known metaphor Jesus gives for this process is the picture of a stubborn, rebellious, foolish son who squanders his inheritance and blows up his life. At his lowest moment, he thinks about his home and his father and how life as a servant in his home would be much better than the life he made for himself.

He heads for home in the hopes of the life of a servant and, to his astonishment, finds his loving father waiting for him. The father receives him as his lost beloved child and restores him to his family.

He had squandered his rights. He could make no demand for acceptance. All he could hope for was the grace and kindness of his father.

Not all of God's children come back home. Some decide they'd rather be miserable and in charge than humble themselves and receive His love. Others struggle with whether it's right for the Father to forgive sin.

But every human being who's right with God comes on the basis of what they've been given through Jesus, not what they earned on their own.

It took them awhile, but the disciples figured this out.

This was the message they received and the message they preached.

This is what has allowed billions of people around the world to enter into a relationship with God.

> And this same relationship is available to you right now. Right now, in this moment, in your own words, you can simply say, "Jesus, I want to be close to You. I realize I'll never be good enough to earn my way to You. I repent of my sin—the poor choices I've made. I acknowledge my need for a Savior. I love You and I want to follow You as the Lord of my life."

If you prayed that prayer, God answered it. The Bible says that all those who call upon the name of the Lord will be saved.[1] This doesn't mean once they die—it's much better than that.

Jesus said that if anyone loved Him, they would obey what He said. That's His love language. But He promised

[1] "...for, 'Everyone who calls on the name of the Lord will be saved'" (Romans 10:13, NIV).

that both He and His Father would come and make His home in the life of anyone who believed.[2]

I would also encourage you to follow Jesus' example and be water baptized. This is an outward demonstration of an inward change. It's a celebration. But it's more than that. It doesn't earn your way into heaven but it does help you get closer to Jesus.

You've been received into God's family. Every family needs a home. If you're not already a part of one, I encourage you to find a local church that values and honors God's Word. Jump in and serve. Don't just go to be entertained. Go be a part of what God's doing in the lives of His people.

Each of these steps will help you get closer to Jesus, but there's more. If this little book has inspired you, I would encourage you to read your Bible every day. The consistency is more important than the duration, especially at the beginning. I'd rather you read the Bible 5-10 minutes every day than an hour one day a week.

One of the best ways to learn about the Bible is to read it with other people. You can do this with your family, or if you're single, with your roommates. The goal is to continue to integrate God's Word into the areas of your

[2] "Jesus replied, 'Anyone who loves me will obey my teaching. My Father will love them, and we will come to them and make our home with them'" (John 14:23, NIV).

life that often feel distant from spiritual life. As you do this, you'll feel closer to Jesus.

Another great way to do this is to participate in a small group. Remember, whatever we focus on we get full of. My prayer for you is that you continue to develop an appetite to know more and more about Jesus, and this is an excellent way to keep growing.

For some of you, each of these steps is familiar. You've done them all. But I'm not finished yet. There's one more stage in this journey—one more step Jesus calls every one of us to.

When I was in the Garden of Gethsemane, I remembered that Jesus checked on His closest disciples to see if they were praying for Him. All three times they were sleeping. Later, in Acts 2, the Bible tells us they were devoted to prayer.

What happened? They got in the game. They went from simply *being* Jesus' disciples to making disciples. There's a huge difference between those two things.

It's easy to fall asleep when Jesus asks you to pray if you're only thinking about yourself. But when you're trying to lead someone else, no one has to convince you how much you need prayer.

Jesus' call to go and make disciples wasn't just to His original group or to pastors and church staff. In fact, Ephesians 4 makes it clear this group of vocational ministers exists to empower and equip common everyday people to do the work of the ministry.[3]

It's for everyone.

Now I know what you're thinking: *Okay, Jeff, where do you find them?* Great question. Here's the simple answer: All you need to make a disciple is to find someone who wants to get closer to Jesus and who is a few steps behind you in the process.

If you're a parent, start in your own home.

Honestly, there's no shortage of potential people around you. And if you feel intimidated, remember it's not on you. You'd be surprised to realize the people around you who would be willing if someone invited them to take a closer look.

Don't go up and say, "Do you want to be my disciple?"[4]

[3] "So Christ himself gave the apostles, the prophets, the evangelists, the pastors and teachers, to equip his people for works of service, so that the body of Christ may be built up until we all reach unity in the faith and in the knowledge of the Son of God and become mature, attaining to the whole measure of the fullness of Christ" (Ephesians 4:11-13, NIV).

[4] By the way, they're not "our" disciples; we want them to follow Jesus!

Instead, ask them what they think about Jesus and if they'd like to know more. Then you could take them through this little book together and discuss each chapter. There are sample questions in the back for small groups but they'll work just as well for one-on-one conversations.

It will challenge you. It will remind you of your need to pray.

But I promise you, it will help you get closer to Jesus too.

Acknowledgments

One of the most valuable things I've learned over several decades in ministry is that nothing significant happens without a team. The book you hold in your hands was made possible only because I have an incredible group of people who I work with every day to create and deliver meaningful content. And when I recently traveled to Israel to write this book and film videos at these locations, I took a phenomenal team with me. I want to thank a few people in particular who worked on this project with me from start to finish. Without their help it would not have been possible. Jed Walker did the true heavy lifting, as he spent countless hours taking thoughts and ideas and helping to shape them into meaningful words on a page. I'm thankful, not only for his partnership in ministry, but also for his friendship of over 25 years. The look and feel of what you hold in your hands is credited to Blake Campbell—his vision for the entire creative process, from filming in Israel, to the art and design of this book, has been invaluable. Mel Baggett's contribution as a content editor and her attention to detail in maintaining the manuscript was key in creating the final product. Each member of this team was instrumental in functionally seeing this project through to completion. But more importantly, they live and breathe what's on these pages and get up every day with a desire to see people get closer to Jesus.

APPENDIX

Small Group Study Guide

Can I Use CLOSER to Lead a Small Group?

That's a great question—and the answer is yes! I wrote the book with people like you in mind.

Take your study to the next level by discussing with a small group. You and a friend, or you and a group, can dig deeper into the life of Jesus and how it applies to your life.

Honestly, to really grasp and apply this content to your life, taking the time to talk about this with other people is the best way to do it. This is how Jesus and the early Church studied: they gathered together and discussed the concepts they were processing.

In the following pages, you'll find small group questions to help guide you in a dialogue together. Each week you'll find a key verse, a key thought, a series of discussion questions, and one final application question.

You can also encourage the group to look back at the chapter and discuss their own unique takeaways.

These questions are based on the chapters in this book and videos available at closer.milestonechurch.com.

Jeff Little

SMALL GROUP

Week 1

Jesus Calls the Disciples

This week's video and
discussion questions are based on chapter 1.

Key Verse:

"Come, follow me," Jesus said.

Matthew 4:19a (NIV)

Key Thought:

Starting a genuine relationship with Jesus begins with answering the call "Follow me."

Discussion Questions:

1. How does our schedule impact our ability to be close to Jesus?
2. Why is it difficult to feel close to Jesus at work? Does the fact that Jesus showed up at their "office" change the way you think about this?
3. What happened when Simon Peter put his nets back out? How did he respond?
4. When Jesus calls us to follow, does He tell us where we're going? What's the difference between opening a negotiation and offering an invitation?

Application Question: Name one practical thing that makes it difficult to follow Jesus. How can you overcome this?

SMALL GROUP

Week 2

The Greatest Sermon in History

This week's video and
discussion questions are based on chapter 2.

Key Verse:

"But seek first His kingdom and His righteousness, and all these things will be given to you as well."

Matthew 6:33 (NIV)

Key Thought:

Jesus knows what we need and He cares about every detail of our lives—but He knows our lives are better when we focus on Him, not on our needs.

Discussion Questions:

1. What happens when we focus on something?
2. Why is it unhealthy to constantly focus on things that upset us?
3. How do the things we choose to value impact our lives? Name one practical way you see this in your own life.
4. Do you struggle with worry? What is a basic way to describe what happens in our minds when we worry?

Application Question: Think of something you're currently seeking—it could be work related, family related, or part of your personal development. What would it look like for you to focus on Jesus and trust Him to add this to you?

SMALL GROUP

Week 3

How Do You Amaze Jesus?

This week's video and
discussion questions are based on chapter 3.

Key Verse:

When Jesus heard this, he was amazed at him, and turning to the crowd following him, he said, "I tell you, I have not found such great faith even in Israel."

Luke 7:9 (NIV)

Key Thought:

If we want to be close to Jesus, loving and serving people are more important than our background or the information we know. And the motivation to live this way comes from trusting God's goodness instead of our own.

Discussion Questions:

1. What does the term *positional leader* mean? How does it feel to be led by one?
2. Have you ever used your position to manipulate people? If so, why?
3. What made this Roman centurion unique? Why did he amaze Jesus?
4. How does our temptation to focus on what we deserve impact our ability to get close to Jesus?

Application Question: Take a moment and ask Jesus who He wants you to love and serve this week. What are you going to do for them?

SMALL GROUP

Week 4

See. Believe. Worship.

This week's video and
discussion questions are based on chapter 4.

Key Verse:

He replied, "Whether he is a sinner or not, I don't know. One thing I do know. I was blind but now I see!"

John 9:25 (NIV)

Key Thought:

When you see God at work in your life, when you have a genuine relationship with Him, you want to worship and be close to Him.

Discussion Questions:

1. Have you ever felt like you didn't know enough or made too many poor decisions to be close to God? How did this influence your ability to be close to Jesus?
2. Who makes the first move—do people look for an uncaring God or is God constantly working whether we know it or not? How does this change the way we think about Him?
3. Did Jesus have bigger goals for this man than healing? What was Jesus' plan for him?
4. What motivates us to put our trust in Jesus?

Application Question: What makes it difficult for you to worship?

SMALL GROUP

Week 5

Fear and the Other Side

This week's video and
discussion questions are based on chapter 5.

Key Verse:

But Jesus immediately said to them: "Take courage! It is I. Don't be afraid."

Matthew 14:27 (NIV)

Key Thought:

Jesus doesn't eliminate fear from our lives. He gives us the ability to find courage and strength in the middle of our difficult moments.

Discussion Questions:

1. Which of the most common fears are you afraid of: spiders, germs, clowns, flying, snakes, heights, or public speaking? Is your biggest fear not on the list?
2. What's the difference between being afraid and being fearful? Which one do you struggle with?
3. Where did Jesus send the disciples? What happened when they finally got there?
4. Why does Jesus connect dealing with fear to getting to the other side? How does one impact the other?

Application Question: What's the "other side" Jesus is sending you to? What fear is keeping you from getting there?

SMALL GROUP

Week 6

The Question that Demands an Answer

This week's video and
discussion questions are based on chapter 6.

Key Verse:
He said to them, "But who do you say that I am?"
Matthew 16:15 (ESV)

Key Thought:
Every person has to answer Jesus' question: *Who do you say I am*? To answer correctly, we need more than information; we need a revelation of Jesus.

Discussion Questions:
1. Why was Caesarea Philippi a surprising setting for this story? What did Jesus mean by the "Gates of Hell"?
2. How did Peter know the answer? What did Jesus say to him when he answered correctly?
3. Does Peter's answer hold up to historical scrutiny? How do we know that Jesus was more than a prophet or a teacher?
4. What does Jesus want us to know? How does this impact our ability to be close to Him?

Application Question: What's the difference between knowing about Jesus and knowing Jesus? Do you have a revelation of Jesus?

SMALL GROUP

Week 7

Servant King, Risen Lord

This week's video and
discussion questions are based on chapter 7.

Key Verse:

For what I received I passed on to you as of first importance: that Christ died for our sins according to the Scriptures, that he was buried, that he was raised on the third day according to the Scriptures.

1 Corinthians 15:3-4 (NIV)

Key Thought:

Jesus didn't come to give self-righteous people a little help, or to make bad people good. Jesus came to bring dead people back to life.

Discussion Questions:

1. What does the Passover have to do with the cross and the resurrection? Did the disciples understand this?
2. How does what Jesus did in the Garden of Gethsemane relate to what happened in the Garden in Genesis 3? Did they take Jesus' life or did He lay it down?
3. Why did so many of Jesus' own people fail to see Him for who He was?
4. What does Jesus tell us through the cross and the empty tomb? Could we be close to God without what happened there?

Application Question: How do the cross and the empty tomb give us practical hope today?

SMALL GROUP

Week 8

Close to the Purpose, Close to the Person

This week's video and
discussion questions are based on chapter 8.

Key Verse:

Therefore go and make disciples of all nations.

Matthew 28:19a (NIV)

Key Thought:

Jesus empowers and invites us to join Him in His mission. If you want to stay close to His person, you have to stay close to His purpose.

Discussion Questions:

1. What is peak-end theory? Have you experienced this in your own life?
2. How do Luke 24 and Acts 1–2 describe the explosive start of the Church?
3. What was the mission Jesus gave His disciples? Was it just for them or was it for any of His followers?
4. How do you know if someone is a disciple?

Application Question: Can we change anyone? What does Jesus promise to anyone willing to join His purpose?

VISIT US ONLINE

MILESTONECHURCH.COM

CONNECT WITH JEFF LITTLE

@JEFFLITTLE

@JEFF_LITTLE

@PASTORJEFFLITTLE